Editor
Eric Migliaccio

Editor in Chief
Ina Massler Levin, M.A.

Creative Director
Karen J. Goldfluss, M.S. Ed.

Illustrator
Mark Mason

Cover Artist
Barb Lorseyedi

Art Coordinator
Renée Mc Elwee

Imaging
James Edward Grace
Rosa C. See

Publisher
Mary D. Smith, M.S. Ed.

FOLLOWING DIRECTIONS

GRADE **3**

VERBAL

WRITTEN

PHYSICAL

Teach Students to
- understand and follow verbal, physical, and written directions.
- read closely and listen carefully.
- work individually, with partners, and in groups.

Author

Susan Mackey Collins, M.Ed.

Teacher Created Resources

6421 Industry Way
Westminster, CA 92683
www.teachercreated.com

ISBN: 978-1-4206-8713-2

© 2012 Teacher Created Resources
Made in U.S.A.

Teacher Created Resources

Table of Contents

Introduction

All students need to be able to successfully follow directions. The ability to follow directions is a lifelong skill that must be practiced and continuously developed. Learning this skill can help a child be successful not only in his or her academics, but also in the time he or she spends outside of the learning environment of school. Learning the skills required to follow directions is essential to success in all areas of life.

Why is it important to place such an emphasis on the skills needed to follow directions? Because directions truly are everywhere, they are a part of daily life. Playing a game, reading a map, putting together a toy, cooking from a recipe, completing an assignment—all require the ability to correctly follow directions. Students who are skilled at following directions most often have also mastered the art of listening. Listening skills are a key element in following directions. Students must pay attention to details in directions with both written and oral information.

Following Directions: Grade 3 is written to help facilitate and increase a student's ability to focus on and follow different types of directions in a variety of academic areas. This book is an invaluable resource that is divided into three main sections:

> **Verbal and Physical Directions**

> **Writing and Written Directions**

> **Partners and Groups**

Each section of this book stresses the importance of developing the skills needed to follow directions accurately. The worksheets and activities in the book guide the students through various levels of performance as well as the key elements of following directions.

The worksheets and activities in *Following Directions: Grade 3* can be completed in any order. A teacher or parent can start working at the beginning of the book and work through to the end of the book, or he or she can choose to skip through the activities and complete different pages in the various sections. No matter which order is used, the skills gained from the lessons in this book will be a great asset to any student.

Now there is nothing left to do but get started, and that's a direction that is fun and easy to follow!

Meeting Standards

Each lesson in *Following Directions: Grade 3* meets one or more of the following standards, which are used with permission from McREL.

Copyright 2011, McREL, Mid-continent Research for Education and Learning.
Address: 4601 DTC Boulevard, Suite 500, Denver, CO 80237.
Telephone: 303-337-0990. Website: *www.mcrel.org/standards-benchmarks.*

Note: To align McREL standards to the Common Core Standards, go to *www.mcrel.org.*

Standards and Benchmarks	Page #
Effectively uses mental processes that are based on similarities and differences ✛ Understands that one way to make sense of something is to think how it is like something more familiar	6, 14
Displays effective interpersonal communication skills ✛ Uses nonverbal communication such as eye contact, body position, and gesture effectively	7, 12, 17
Demonstrates perseverance ✛ Concentrates mental and physical energies to meet the demands of the task ✛ Persists in the face of difficulty	8, 12, 17, 21–27, 32, 36 31, 40, 42, 45–46
Understands the social and personal responsibility associated with participation in physical activity ✛ Understands the physical challenges faced by people with disabilities	9
Understands and applies the basic principles of presenting an argument ✛ Asks questions about and seeks better reasons for believing arguments than the assertion that "everybody knows" or "I just know"	10, 18
Knows how to use structures and functions of art ✛ Uses structures and functions of art to communicate ideas	11
Knows a range of subject matter, symbols, and potential ideas in the visual arts ✛ Knows how subject matter, symbols, and ideas are used to communicate meaning	12
Understands the characteristics and uses of maps, globes, and other geographic tools and technologies ✛ Knows the basic elements of maps and globes	13

Meeting Standards *(cont.)*

Standards and Benchmarks	Page #
Uses listening and speaking strategies for different purposes ✢ Uses a variety of verbal communication skills	15
Understands and applies basic and advanced properties of the concepts of geometry ✢ Understands basic properties of figures	16, 33
Uses a variety of strategies in the problem-solving process ✢ Understands that some ways of representing a problem are more helpful than others ✢ Uses a variety of strategies to understand problem situations	17 38
Understands the structure and function of cells and organisms ✢ Knows that living organisms have distinct structures and body systems that serve specific functions in growth, survival, and reproduction	19
Understands relationships among organisms and their physical environment ✢ Knows the organization of simple food chains and food webs	20, 39
Uses the stylistic and rhetorical aspects of writing ✢ Uses a variety of sentence structures in writing ✢ Uses descriptive and precise language that clarifies and enhances ideas	27 36, 43–44
Uses basic and advanced procedures while performing the processes of computation ✢ Multiplies and divides whole numbers	28
Uses general skills and strategies of the writing process ✢ Uses strategies to write for a variety of purposes	29
Uses grammatical and mechanical conventions in written compositions ✢ Writes in cursive	30
Understands the composition and structure of the universe and the Earth's place in it ✢ Knows that night and day are caused by the Earth's rotation on its axis	34
Understands selected attributes and historical developments of societies in Africa, the Americas, Asia, and Europe ✢ Knows about life in urban areas and communities of various cultures of the world at various times in their histories	37
Understands and applies the basic and advanced properties of the concepts of measurement ✢ Selects and uses appropriate tools for given measurement situations	41

Follow Directions Effectively

Directions: Follow each direction to create a new picture in the section or sections described.

1. Draw two eyes, a nose, and a mouth inside the circle in section B.

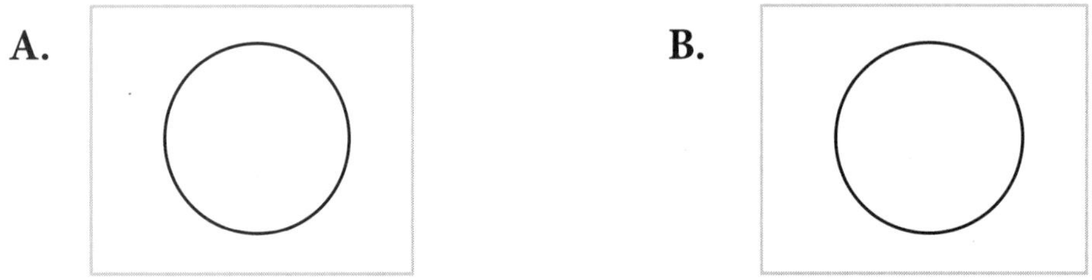

2. Add two more circles on top of the circle in section A. Then copy your drawing from box A to box B. Add extra details to create a snowman in box B.

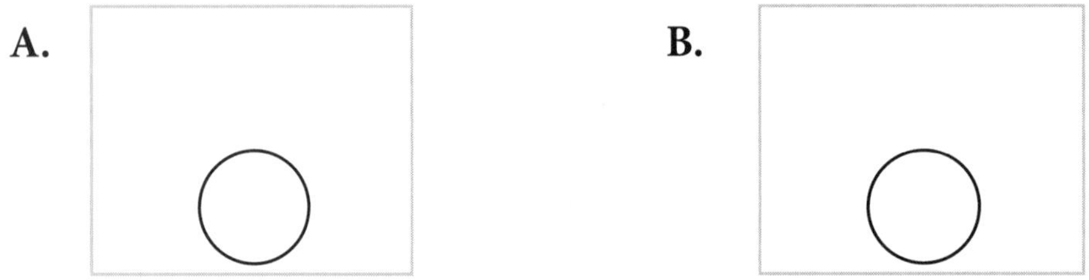

3. Use the triangle shape in section A to draw a sailboat. Use the triangle shape in section B to draw a clown's hat.

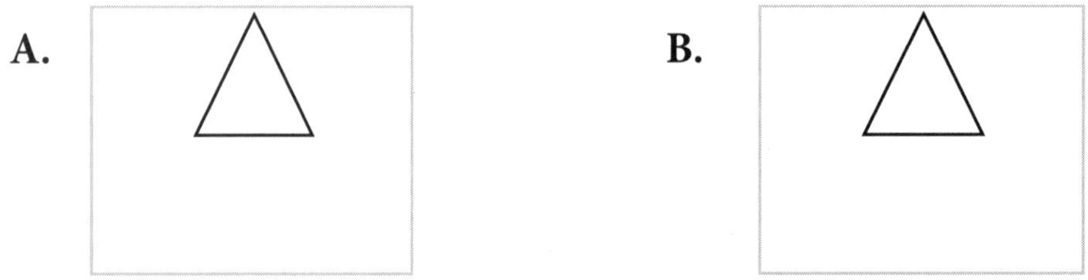

4. Draw a triangle on top of the rectangles in both section A and section B. Add details so each picture looks like a house; however, the house in section A cannot look exactly like the house in section B.

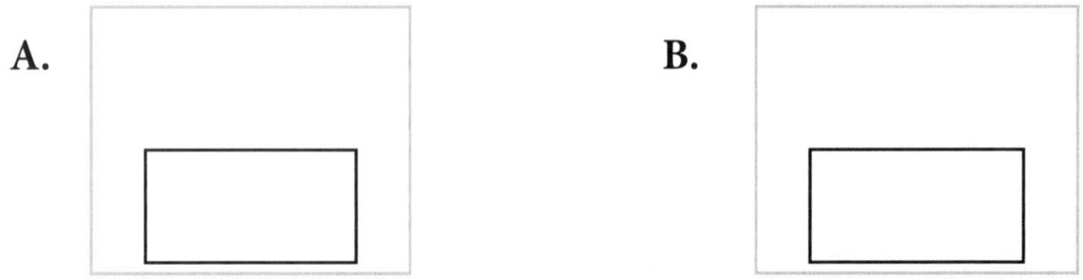

Physical Directions Without Talking

Directions: Divide the class into two equal groups. (If there is an odd number of students, have volunteers swap out and act as scorekeepers.)

Groups will compete to be the first to successfully complete each task. One point goes to the group that successfully completes the task first. Choose tasks, in any order, from the list below. Each group must complete each task, even if the other group has already completed it.

Explain to the students to listen as you give each direction. Once a direction is given, the students will, without talking, communicate with the members of the group to complete each task correctly and as quickly as possible.

List of possible tasks:

1. Everyone in the group will get his or her pencil and then line the pencils up from longest to shortest.

2. Everyone in the group will remove one shoe and line up from largest shoe size to smallest shoe size.

3. Everyone in the group will line up from longest hair to shortest hair.

4. Everyone in the group will line up by eye color where students with the same eye color are grouped together before changing to the next eye color.

5. Everyone in the group will line up by birthday months, starting with the earliest month in the calendar year.

6. Everyone in the group will line up by alphabetical order of his or her last name.

7. Everyone in the group will line up by those who are wearing shoes with laces that tie to those who are not wearing shoes with laces that tie.

Create two tasks of your own:

8. Everyone will _____

9. Everyone will _____

Don't
Do This, Don't Do That

Many activities on following directions explain all the things one should do. This activity is all about the things one shouldn't do!

Directions: Read each direction to the students. Watch carefully to see if each student follows each direction correctly. Remind students to listen for you to read each statement out loud and to carefully follow each direction since directions will not be repeated.

1. Do not sit down.

2. Do not stand on both feet while standing.

3. Do not keep your eyes open.

4. Do not keep your eyes closed.

5. Do not continue to stand.

6. Do not keep your head still.

7. Do not keep moving your head.

8. Do not keep your head off your desk.

9. Do not keep your hands off your desk.

10. Do not keep your feet from tapping.

11. Do not keep your head on your desk.

12. Do not keep your feet tapping.

13. Do not leave your fingers still.

14. Do not continue to move your fingers.

15. Do not keep your hands on your desk.

16. Do not continue to sit.

Working with Differences

Following physical directions is not always easy for those with special disabilities. Use the activities below to better understand how a physical disability can have an effect on the way a person follows a direction.

Part 1 Directions: Many people have arthritis. Arthritis causes a person to have a hard time doing things other people often take for granted—such as holding a pencil, working on a keyboard, or sending a text on a telephone.

Imagine you have arthritis in your hands. Close your fingers so that your hands make a fist. Pick up your pencil between your fingers while your hands remain closed into fists. **Hint:** This "fist position" shows you how hard it would be to write if you had arthritis in your hands.

Once you have your pencil in hand, use your best handwriting and write your name and address on the lines below.

Name: _____

Address: _____

_____

Part 2 Directions: Some people have slight problems with their vision. Some people are completely blind. Imagine you no longer have your eyesight. In the space below, you will need to write your first name and last, but your eyes must be closed while you write.

Think About It: Can having a physical disability make it harder to follow a direction? Do people need to be patient and try to help those who have a physical disability? Why or why not? Write your answers on the back of this page.

Listening to Verbal Directions

Directions: Have each student take out a piece of paper and write the numbers 1–10 on it. Then read each statement below out loud. Tell students to listen as each statement is read. Statements will not be repeated. After each statement is read, the students should answer each question with something they believe is true. (Let the students know ahead of time that their answers will be shared with the class.) Give the students a minute or two to write an answer to each question before proceeding to the next question.

After all of the students have had the time and opportunity to write an answer to each question, share the answers out loud. Each student who has an answer unlike anyone else's in the class will receive a point. Students will not receive a point if someone else in the class has the same answer as them.

To keep score, students should keep up with their own number of points. At the end of the game, each student should total his or her points to determine a winner for the class.

I Just Know . . .

_____ **1.** I just know that today is _____ .

_____ **2.** I just know that most cars have _____ .

_____ **3.** I just know that tennis shoes are made so people can _____ .

_____ **4.** I just know that toast can be made in a/an _____ .

_____ **5.** I just know the best season is _____ .

_____ **6.** I just know my favorite pet is _____ .

_____ **7.** I just know dark clouds can bring _____ .

_____ **8.** I just know cats are different than dogs because _____ .

_____ **9.** I just know Friday is a good day of the week because _____ .

_____ **10.** I just know that recess time is _____ ..

Remind students to total their points after all responses have been read.

Taking Artistic Direction

Materials Needed: crayons

Directions: Follow the directions given for each picture.

1. Draw a smile on the face of the girl. Color the petals on the flowers yellow. Draw a smile on the face of the boy. Color the trunk of the tree brown. Color the top of the tree green.

2. Color the mom's hair red. Color the baby's hair yellow. Draw stripes on the baby's stroller. Color the bottle purple. Draw a bow in the baby's hair.

3. Draw a grin on the girl's face. Color the girl's overalls blue. Draw a moustache on the father's face. Draw a fishing pole in the father's hand. Color the fish gray.

4. Draw mouths on each snowman. Draw a hat on each snowman. Color one hat purple. Color one snowman red. Draw a rabbit between the two snowmen.

Moving with Symbols

Directions: Below are pictures or symbols. Each symbol has a number. Listen as your teacher calls out a number. (Numbers may be called out in random order.) As the teacher says a number out loud, look at the symbol that matches the number. When the number is read out loud, act out the action each symbol represents.

Hint: You may have to stand, move, walk, talk, etc., to act out each symbol.

1.

2.

3.

4.

5.

6.

7.

8. ALLOWED

Getting Around the Town

Materials Needed: red crayon, blue crayon

Directions: Mary needs to get to the pet store on Palm Ave to buy food for her fish. Read the directions below and look at the map. Use a blue crayon to trace the route Mary should take to get to the store. Place a red X on the areas of the map Mary should avoid.

As you leave Mary's house and walk along Willow St., you'll have a choice of two roads to turn on. One road has no sidewalks and goes by Mr. Hill's house, where two mean-looking dogs are often loose in the front yard. This route is on Maple St. The other leads down a nice sidewalk on Oak Ave. However, if Mary takes Oak Ave., it dead-ends. On the way to the dead-end of Oak Ave., there are two streets. Cherry Rd. is on the left, and it takes you straight to the pet store. You must pass through a dangerous railroad crossing to get there, though. The other choice is Hickory Ln. on the right. It is a bit longer, but it has nice sidewalks and no railroad to cross.

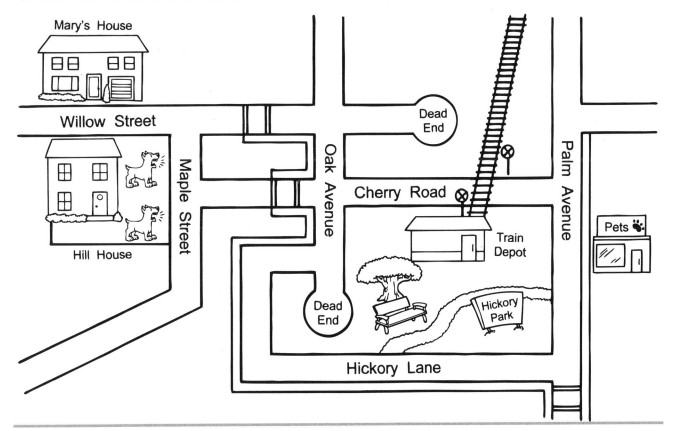

Write It Out: Pretend you need to give a friend directions from Mary's house to the pet store. Write the directions that would be the safest route. Use the back of the page.

Following From "Left" to "Write"

Directions: Have each student crumple a sheet of paper and hold the wad of paper in his or her right hand. As you read the story below out loud to the class, the students must listen carefully for two words: "leftovers" and "write." Each time they hear the word "leftovers," they must move the wad of paper to their left hand. If the paper wad is already in their left hand when they hear the word "leftovers," they should place their paper wad on the desktop in front of them. Each time the students hear the word "write," they should place the wad of paper in their right hand. If the paper is already in their right hand when they hear the word "write," they should place the wad of paper on the desktop in front of them.

The Directions Story

Katie hated eating leftovers after Thanksgiving, but she knew her family would have leftovers for several nights whether she wanted them or not. She thought about getting on the computer so she could write a report for her English class that was due after the holidays. She could write about why she hated eating leftovers. She could write about all the clever uses her mother had for the leftovers of turkey. She could write about the disgusting leftovers her mother would serve for breakfast for the next two weeks. Really, she could probably write and write and write for days about eating horrible leftovers. Katie sighed. She did not want to write about anything. She was so full that she really just wanted to take a nap, but she knew if she took a nap she would wake up hungry. And when she woke up, the only thing her mother would offer for her supper was leftovers! Katie went ahead and took her nap. As she napped, she dreamed about leftovers that were chasing her and threatening to eat her! Katie jumped out of bed and went straight to her computer to write. She knew she would have to write down her dream or she would forget it. She couldn't wait to tell about her dream at supper. She would entertain her family with her crazy dream while they all feasted on leftovers!

Questions to Share With the Class:

- Was the activity hard to do? Why or why not?con

- What are some skills needed to be successful at this activity?

Sing It Out Loud

Follow the directions carefully to complete this fun activity.

Directions: Using the tune to "Twinkle, Twinkle, Little Star" or any other familiar children's song, write lyrics to the music to explain something you might have learned in school. Choose from the list below.

- proper and common nouns
- the eight parts of speech
- figurative language

- learning your times tables (4s, 5s, 6s, etc.)
- liquid measurements
- the names of 3-D shapes

Once you have written your song, you must teach the song to at least two other classmates. Volunteers may be asked to perform songs, so if you are shy, one of your classmates just might be able to perform your song for you!

> **Example:**
>
> **"All About Nouns"**
>
> (*sung to the tune of "Twinkle, Twinkle, Little Star"*)
>
> Proper, common — nouns, nouns, nouns
>
> Nouns are seen all over towns
>
> Capitalize all proper nouns
>
> Lowercase all common nouns
>
> Proper nouns are always specific
>
> Common nouns are plain but terrific!

Title of my song: _____

Sung to the tune of _____

Drawing with Symmetry

Items that are symmetrical can be folded in half so that the two parts are the same and match exactly.

Look at this picture of a butterfly. Now fold this piece of paper in half so the fold goes up the center, dotted line located on the butterfly's body. Unfold the paper and notice that on each side of the fold, the butterfly is identical or symmetrical

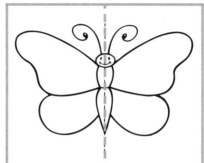

Directions: Draw the other half of each picture below so that each one is perfectly symmetrical.

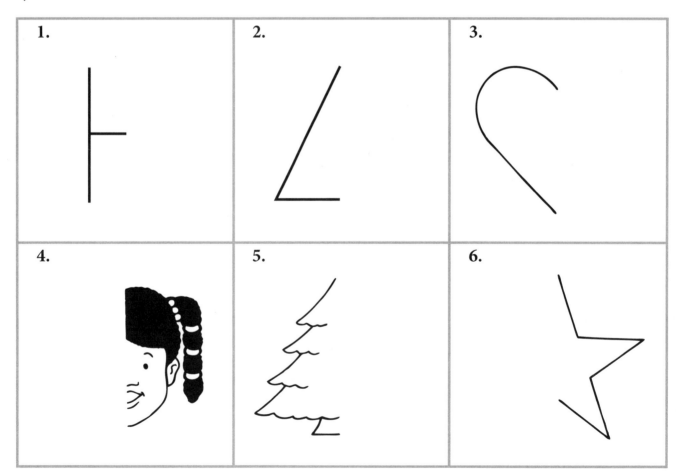

Creating Living Clocks

Student Directions: Stand beside your desk. Listen as your teacher calls out a specific time of day from the list below. Times can be called out in any order.

As your teacher calls out a time, use your arms to represent the hands on a clock. Change arms as needed to represent the long and short hands of the clock.

Hint: It does not matter if the time is A.M. or P.M.

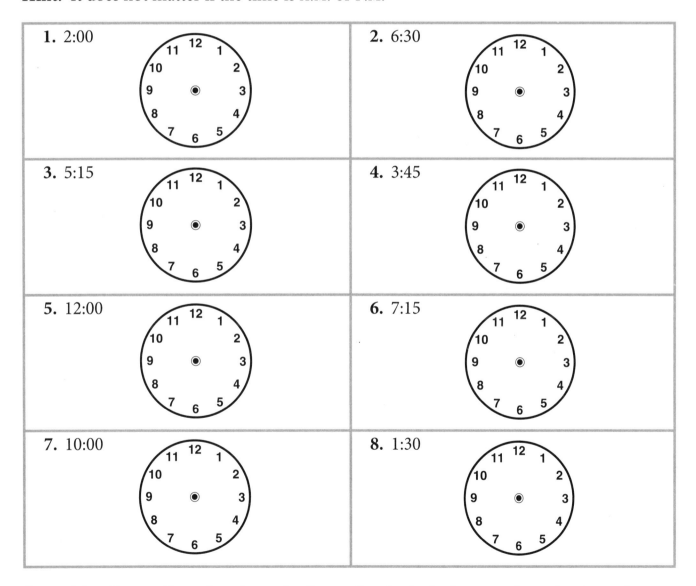

1. 2:00	**2.** 6:30
3. 5:15	**4.** 3:45
5. 12:00	**6.** 7:15
7. 10:00	**8.** 1:30

Something Extra: Draw hands on the faces of each clock above to show the times that are listed.

Following Directions to Support Your Ideas

Directions: Prepare information for an oral report. Gather information for the oral report to explain the importance of recycling. Find information to support this belief by using the following verbal and nonverbal resources. Follow the directions in the order they are given.

1. Use a book to find information supporting the importance of recycling.

   Title of the book: _____

   Name of the author: _____

   An important fact from the book: _____

   _____

2. Interview a classmate to find out why he or she believes it is important to recycle.

   What you have learned: _____

   _____

   Name of person interviewed: _____

3. Find an article or advertisement from a newspaper or magazine (or other daily, weekly, or monthly news source) that supports the importance of recycling. List at least two important facts about recycling on the lines provided.

   _____

   _____

Use the information you gathered to create a flyer about the importance of recycling. Present the information on your flyer to the class to help persuade everyone how important it is to recycle. Follow these additional directions for your flyer:

- The flyer must be drawn on a white 8 ½" x 11" piece of paper.

- The flyer must be colored with crayons or colored pencils.

- The flyer must contain information you learned from answering the questions above.

Can You Color the Parts of a Plant?

Materials Needed: yellow crayon, green crayon, brown crayon, orange crayon

Directions: Read the entire page before you begin coloring any part of the picture. Use what you know about the parts of a plant to correctly color the parts.

Part 1 Directions:

- Color the flower yellow.
- Color the stem orange.

- Color the leaves green.
- Color the roots brown.

Part 2 Directions: Do not color the parts of the plant using the directions in Part I. Do use the colors listed below to color the picture of the plant.

- Color the flower orange.
- Color the stem green.

- Color the leaves brown.
- Color the roots yellow.

If you colored your picture by the directions in Part I, draw the picture of the plant on a separate sheet of paper. Then color the picture using the directions in Part II.

Listen and Learn About Food Chains

Directions: Have each student stand beside his or her desk. (For students unable to stand, many of the physical directions can be easily adapted, or students can write answers to the questions on paper.)

Explain to the students they will need to listen as you read several statements about food chains. Students should correctly respond to each direction that is given and then stop and listen when the teacher begins each new statement.

Visually check to see if students understand each verbal direction. Check to see if students understand the science concept.

Statements

1. Take one step forward if an herbivore eats plants.

2. Hop on one foot if an omnivore eats only meat.

3. Pat your stomach with one hand if a food chain shows how living organisms are connected.

4. Clap your hands three times if a decomposer breaks down leftover food.

5. Take one step back if an organism's home is also known as its habitat.

6. Sit down if a food chain shows that living things are not connected.

7. Stomp your feet if all living things need energy.

8. Pat your head if an animal that eats both meat and plants is called an omnivore.

9. Use your fingers to wiggle your nose if a consumer is an organism that makes its own energy.

10. Clap and cheer because science rocks!

Listen to Directions and Draw

Materials Needed: paper, pencil

Directions: Students will listen to and carefully follow the verbal directions given by you. When all the directions have been given, the students will have drawn a picture that looks like the picture found in the answer key (see page 47).

Directions for Students

Listen carefully to each direction. Wait until I finish reading each direction before you begin drawing. I will read each direction only once, and I will then give you time to follow the direction I have just read. I will not repeat the direction.

1. Draw one circle in the center of the page. The circle should be about the size of a checker from a game of checkers.

2. Draw a second circle to the right of the first circle. It should be the same size as the first circle, and it should be touching the edge of the first circle. The two circles should be side-by-side.

3. Draw a third circle on top of the two circles you have already drawn. This circle should be between the other circles, and it should touch both of them. This third circle should be about the size of your thumbnail.

4. Draw a circle about a half of an inch above the first circle you drew. The new circle should be the size of your thumbnail. The circle should not touch any of the other circles.

5. Shade in the circle you just drew.

6. Draw a circle about a half of an inch above the second circle you drew. The new circle should be the size of your thumbnail. The circle should not touch any of the other circles.

7. Shade in the circle you just drew.

8. Draw one triangle above each shaded circle. The triangles should be about the size of your nose. The triangles should not touch the circles.

9. Draw a curved line that starts at the bottom of your first circle and ends at the bottom of your second circle. This curved line should be shaped like the letter "U."

Compare pictures to find out how well the students did.

Playing "Teacher Says"

Directions: Students will listen carefully as the teacher gives a set of directions. Students will only follow the direction given if the words "the teacher says" are given before the direction. Use the list provided on page 23. The directions do not have to be given in any specific order; however, they can be read in the order they are listed.

To begin the game, have students stand in a line or beside their desks.

Read the following directions to your students before beginning:

Rules of the Game

Students, I am going to read a set of directions aloud to you.

1. Only follow the direction I have read if it begins with the words "the teacher says."

2. If you miss a direction, you must sit down wherever you are standing. You must remain seated while two more directions are given. After two directions have been given, you can rejoin the game.

Teacher Suggestions:

- Add your own directions that will work well with your own class.

- Before beginning the game, remind each student that he or she is on the honor system and must sit down even if the teacher does not say anything to him or her.

- As the activity continues, increase the speed of the game by reading the directions more quickly.

- At the end of the game, be sure to recognize any students who followed all directions correctly.

Playing "Teacher Says" *(cont.)*

"Teacher Says" List

1. Pat your stomach with your right hand.
2. The teacher says pat your stomach with your right hand.
3. The teacher says pat your head with your left hand.
4. The teachers says stop patting your stomach and your head.
5. The teacher says spin in a circle.
6. The teacher says stop spinning in a circle.
7. Hop on one foot.
8. The teacher says run in place.
9. The teacher says hop on both feet.
10. The teacher says stop.
11. The teacher says tap one foot.
12. Stop tapping.
13. The teacher says stop tapping your foot.
14. The teacher says "moo" like a cow.
15. The teacher says "crow" like a rooster.
16. The teacher says "bark" like a dog.
17. "Oink" like a pig.
18. The teacher says stop barking like a dog.
19. The teacher says cover your eyes.
20. Uncover your eyes.
21. The teacher says uncover your eyes.
22. The teacher says nod your head.
23. The teacher says blink your eyes.
24. The teacher says stop nodding your head.
25. The teacher says stop blinking your eyes.
26. The teacher says to say your first name over and over.
27. The teacher says to stop saying your first name.
28. The teacher says to wave to the person beside you.
29. The teacher says to stop waving to the person beside you.
30. The teacher says to shout only once, "I love following directions!"

Write Out the Directions

Directions: Look at each picture in Column A. Notice the pictures in Column B are different than the pictures in Column A. Write directions for picture ideas for Column C. Explain what you can draw to add more details to the picture.

Hint: You are writing what could be drawn; you are not drawing a picture in Column C.

	Column A	Column B	Column C
Example:			Draw a worm sticking its head out of the hole in the apple.
1.			
2.			
3.			
4.			
5.			

Writing a Recipe for Fun

People use recipes to help create certain dishes. For example, if someone wants to make brownies, he follows the directions needed to make the special chocolate treat. Recipes are written directions for cooks to follow to have success with their cooking.

Now it's your turn to write a "different" type of recipe.

Directions: Use the recipe card below to write a recipe for fun. Think of something you like to do. Now imagine you have to write directions or a recipe for someone to follow to enjoy your fun activity. Try to complete your recipe in five easy steps. Be specific, just like a real recipe, and be sure to give your recipe card a title!

Recipe: _____

Step 1: _____
_____

Step 2: _____
_____

Step 3: _____
_____

Step 4: _____
_____

Step 5: _____
_____

Something Extra: Make a recipe card on the back of this page. Write a recipe for your favorite dish.

Reading Written Directions

Written directions are easy to understand if you take the time to carefully read what is written. The great thing about written directions is you do not have to remember what was said. The directions are all written on a piece of paper. All you have to do is read them!

Practice what you know about written directions by completing the following activity.

Directions: Read each written direction. Complete each one.

1. Write your first and last name on the line: _____

2. Draw a circle around your name.

3. Do not write an answer to this question: What is your favorite animal?

   _____

4. Do not draw a picture of a flower in the space to the right.

5. Write today's date using only numbers. _____

6. Write your teacher's name on the blank line for question #6.

   Monday, Tuesday, _____, Thursday, Friday, Saturday, Sunday

7. Write the names of four animals that have four legs.

   _____, _____,

   _____, _____

8. Do not circle an answer to this question.

My Favorite Flower

Following directions can be

   a. easy   **b.** hard   **c.** sometimes easy; sometimes hard

Writing
Very Urgent Directions!

Directions: Write an exclamatory or imperative sentence to help give a direction.

Example: Write a sentence telling someone to stop running in the school hallways.

Stop running in the halls right now!

1. Write a sentence telling someone to go to the office.

_____

2. Write a sentence telling someone to stop a thief.

_____

3. Write a sentence telling someone to stop making so much noise.

_____

4. Write a sentence telling someone to clean up his or her mess.

_____

5. Write a sentence telling someone to stop talking in the library.

_____

6. Write a sentence telling someone to look out for a slippery spot on the floor.

_____

7. Write a sentence telling someone to stop being mean.

_____

8. Write a sentence telling someone to help you.

_____

Following Written Directions for Math

Part 1 Directions: Multiply to find each product. Only write the answers that have 4 as a factor.

1. 5 x 4 = _____

5. 8 x 7 = _____

9. 12 x 4 = _____

2. 6 x 3 = _____

6. 7 x 7 = _____

10. 2 x 11 = _____

3. 2 x 2 = _____

7. 3 x 9 = _____

11. 1 x 0 = _____

4. 4 x 4 = _____

8. 4 x 8 = _____

12. 10 x 4 = _____

Part 2 Directions: Multiply to find each product. Only write the answers that have 5 as a factor.

13.
```
    5
  x 5
```

17.
```
    9
  x 5
```

21.
```
    8
  x 5
```

14.
```
    7
  x 4
```

18.
```
   10
  x 2
```

22.
```
    2
  x 0
```

15.
```
    6
  x 3
```

19.
```
    3
  x 4
```

23.
```
   11
  x 5
```

16.
```
   12
  x 8
```

20.
```
    5
  x 3
```

24.
```
    6
  x 7
```

Writing Down the Routine

Directions: A new student has moved to your class. He has the same schedule as you. The teacher has asked you to help the new student with the first day at his new school.

Since the new student did not bring his lunch, he needs help with the rules in the cafeteria. He needs help knowing how to buy his lunch. Help your new classmate by writing directions to explain the routine for the school's cafeteria.

When you are finished, let your teacher look at the procedures and rules to see if you have left out anything important.

Remember: Give detailed directions for the student to follow. The new student has never been to your school's cafeteria.

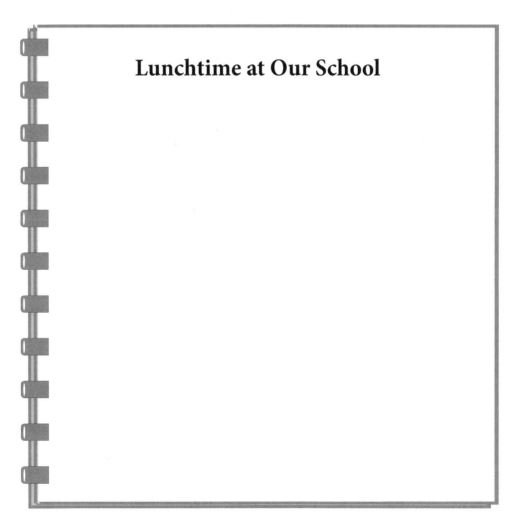

Lunchtime at Our School

Paying Attention to What's Written

Written directions must be read carefully. Written directions in school can help a student correctly complete an assignment.

Directions: Follow the written directions given below to complete the assignment.

1. Underline each lowercase letter *c*. Do not underline any whole words.

   C   c   C   c   cat   cat   cat

2. Circle the cursive letters. Trace the words.

   Y   *y*   *Y*   y   *yak yak yak*

3. Trace the cursive letters. Write a word on the line that begins with the letter that is given.

   S   s   S   s   _____

4. Trace the cursive letters. Write a word on the line that begins with a different letter than the one that is given.

   W   w   W   w   _____

5. Trace the cursive letter. Write the letter four times.

   q   _____

6. Do nothing to the word *apple*.

   apple   apple   apple   apple   apple   _____

7. Write the word *grape* before each word that says *juice*.

   juice   juice   juice   _____

Social Studies Information Hunt

Directions: Read the entire page before you begin. You will have 10 minutes to find as many answers as you can to the questions below. Use your social studies textbook, the Internet (with teacher permission), or any other easily available resource, if needed, to help find the answers.

1. What was the first successful colony established in America?

   _____

2. What colony is known as the "lost colony"?

   _____

3. Jamestown was located in what present-day state?

   _____

4. The ship the Pilgrims arrived on was called the

   _____ .

5. Color the picture of the *Mayflower*.

6. The Pilgrims sailed to the Americas from the

   country of _____

   to be free to practice their own religion.

7. The Pilgrims settled in what present-day state? _____

8. Which famous colony was founded in 1607? _____

After reading all of the questions, write your name in the top right corner of this page. Then answer question #4. Do not answer any other questions on this page. Do not write anything except your name and the answer to question #4. When you are finished, sit quietly until everyone else is done.

What If It's Different?

Sometimes people think they already know how to do something, so they do not read the directions. If a teacher gives you written directions, always carefully read them. It is very important to follow directions exactly as they are written.

Read and follow each direction that is given.

Part 1 Directions: Do not draw a line to match each person to his or her description.

1. first President of the United States   **a.** Abraham Lincoln

2. President of the United States   **b.** George Washington

3. helped create the flag of the new
   United States   **c.** Benjamin Franklin

4. famous for his experiment with
   a kite and lightning   **d.** Betsy Ross

Part 2 Directions: Write your first name on each line to complete each sequence.

1. January, February, March, _____

2. Mercury, Venus, Earth, _____

3. spring, summer, winter, _____

Part 3 Directions: Draw a square on the line if the answer to the math problem is an odd number. Draw a triangle on the line if the answer to the math problem is an even number.

1. 5 x 5 = _____   5. 10 x 10 = _____

2. 7 x 4 = _____   6. 9 x 9 = _____

3. 8 x 2 = _____   7. 4 x 4 = _____

4. 6 x 3 = _____   8. 7 x 7 = _____

How Drawing Is Like Writing

Drawing is a type of writing. Ancient Egyptians used hieroglyphics, or pictures, to stand for written words. People throughout the ages have used pictures to express their thoughts and ideas.

Use the exercise below to help practice following directions. Remember, a figure that is symmetrical can be folded in half and each part will match exactly.

Directions: Follow each individual direction that is given.

1. Draw the other half of the dog so that it is symmetrical.

2. Look at the two pictures below. Color the picture that is symmetrical.

3. Draw the other half of the house so that it is symmetrical.

4. Draw the other half of the butterfly so that it is not symmetrical.

5. Use the box with the dotted line to draw a face that is symmetrical. On one side of the dotted line draw half of the face. On the other side of the dotted line draw half of the face. Each half must be symmetrical to the other.

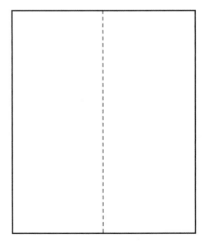

The Earth, the Moon, the Directions

Directions: Read each question fully and follow each direction that is given. Use your textbook, the Internet (with teacher's permission), or any other available resource as needed to help find the correct answers.

1. How long does it take Earth to make a complete rotation?

   (A) 7 days

   (B) 24 hours

   If the correct answer is choice "A," draw a picture of the moon here:

   If the correct answer is choice "B," draw a picture of Earth here:

2. Through how many phases does the moon go?

   (A) eight phases

   (B) six phases

   If the correct answer is choice "A," draw four stars to the right of choice "A."
   If the correct answer is choice "B," draw one star to the right of choice "B."

3. What are the names of the two groups in which the planets in our solar system are divided?

   (A) small and large

   (B) inner and outer

   If the correct answer choice is "A," write the names of the eight planets in our solar system in the box to the right.

   If the correct answer choice is "B," write the names of the first four planets in our solar system in the box to the right.

4. On what does the Earth rotate or spin?

   (A) its axis

   (B) its biosphere

   If the correct answer choice is "A," draw two lines under the correct answer.

   If the correct answer choice is "B," draw three lines under the correct answer.

It's Time
to Learn to Follow Directions

Directions: Read over the entire page before you begin. Look at each clock. Write the time on the line.

1.

_____

2.

_____

3.

_____

4.

_____

5.

_____

6.

_____

7.

_____

8.

_____

9.

_____

Do not write the time for any of the clocks on this worksheet. Leave all of the lines blank. Now look at the clock in the classroom or at your own watch. Draw hands on the clock to the right to show what the time was when you discovered how to follow directions the right way!

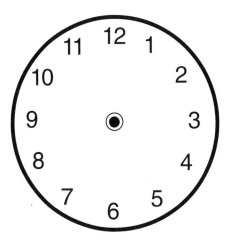

Writing
for the Future

Directions: Pretend you must leave some information in a time capsule for people 200 years in the future. Certain items will be placed in the capsule. You have been asked to write directions to place in the time capsule to explain how to use each item.

1. a belt

How to wear a belt:

_____

_____

_____

2. a toothbrush

How to use a toothbrush:

_____

_____

_____

3. Choose a game you like to play such as leapfrog, tag, or hopscotch. Write the name of the game on the first line provided. Write the directions for how to play the game on the lines below. Draw a picture of the game in the box to the right.

_____

_____

_____

_____

_____

_____

_____

Coloring the Places of the Past

People in the past often lived in communities just like people do in the present. Communities are areas where people live and generally share common interests. Many communities, both past and present, have things in common, such as schools, grocery stores, barber shops, etc.

Directions: Look at the community of the past. Use the chart below to color the picture.

Color Chart

- Color the livery stable **brown**.
- Color the barber shop **blue**.
- Color the dry goods store **gray**.

- Color the school house **red**.
- Color the boarding house **yellow**.

Something Extra: On the back of this page, draw a picture of your community. Label each building in your community. Color the picture when you are finished.

Completing the Pattern

Directions: To complete each pattern, draw what is asked for. Then solve each problem.

1. First, draw 4 more hearts.

   Next, multiply the total number of hearts by 3.

   _____ hearts x 3 = _____ hearts

2. First, draw 7 more triangles.

   Next, multiply the total number of triangles by 5.

   _____ triangles x 5 = _____ triangles

3. First, draw 10 more diamonds.

   Next, multiply the total number of diamonds by 8.

   _____ diamonds x 8 = _____ diamonds

4. First, draw 5 more rectangles.

   Next, multiply the total number of rectangles by 4.

   _____ rectangles x 4 = _____ rectangles

5. First, draw 6 more smiling faces.

   Next, multiply the total number of smiling faces by 2.

   _____ smiling faces x 2 = _____ smiling faces

Herbivores, Carnivores, Omnivores

Herbivores are animals that eat only plants. Carnivores are animals that eat only meat. Omnivores are animals that eat both plants and meat.

Directions: Look at the pictures of the animals below. Color the pictures as follows:

✢ Color the herbivores **green.**   ✢ Color the omnivores **yellow.**

✢ Color the carnivores **blue.**

Hint: Be sure to research any animal you do not know.

Not
What You Want to Do

Directions: Read and follow each instruction.

1. Write the letter A on the line.

   1, 2, 3, 4, _____ , 6, 7, 8, 9, 10

2. How many eggs are in a dozen? Write the answer on the line for question 3.

   _____

3. How old are you? Do not answer this question. _____

4. Draw a circle around each even number in question 1.

5. If you had 5 baseballs and you gave away 4 baseballs, how many soccer balls would you have remaining? If you cannot answer this question with the information you have, write the word "raccoon" on the line.

   _____

6. Stand up in class and clap three times if you think this worksheet is easy.

7. Stand up in class and clap three times if you did not clap on question 6.

8. Write only your first name on the line below.

   _____

9. Write the month you were born. Do this on the line for question 2.

   _____

10. Two kittens chased a mouse under a couch. How many dogs were there? If you can answer this question with the information you have, draw a mouse in the box. If you cannot answer this question with the information you have, draw a triangle in the box.

Following Directions for Measurement

Part 1 Directions: Read the entire page before you begin.

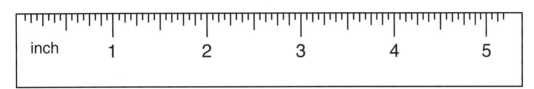

Cut out the ruler above and use it to find the length of each item. Write the length of each item on the line.

1. _____ inches

2. _____ inches

3. _____ inches

Part 2 Directions: Use the ruler to draw rows of smiling faces that are the lengths of the measurements that are given.

4. 2 inches

5. 4 inches

Part 3 Directions: Do not complete Part I or Part II. Write the phrase "I read and follow all directions" on the line below and give this paper to your teacher.

_____

Every Word Is a Step on the Stairs

Directions: Read the first word that is given. Write a word on the next line that begins with the ending letter of the word on the line before it. Continue with this pattern to the end of each set.

octopus

bell

broccoli

sofa

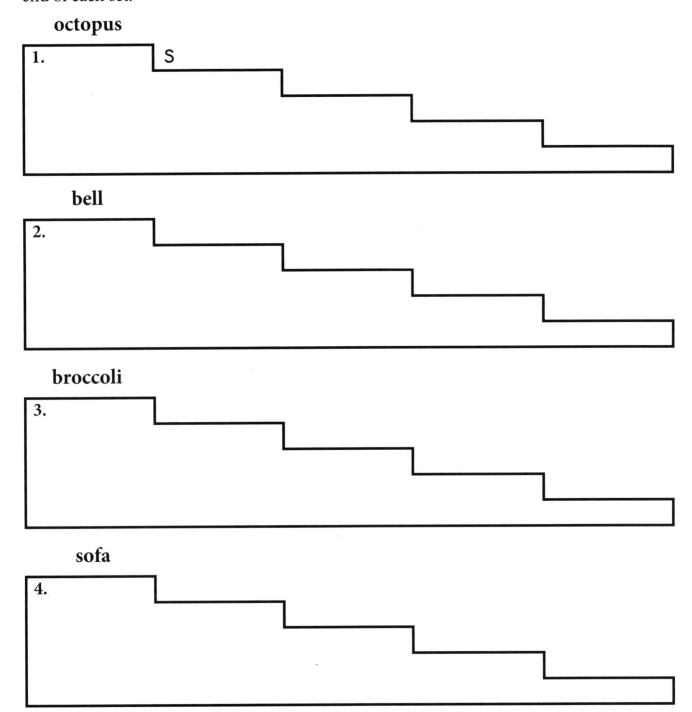

Practice
Writing Directions

Have you ever had a new game for which you had to read the directions to know how to play? Have you ever had a recipe you had to read to know how to make a new dish? In order to do any of these things, you had to be able to follow directions that someone else had written.

Written directions must be clear. Written directions need to thoroughly explain how to do something. When a person writes directions, he or she must pretend the person reading the directions has no idea how to do the activity. The directions he or she writes must be clear and to the point.

Part 1 Directions: Draw a simple picture in the space below. Use only triangles, squares, rectangles, and circles to draw your picture.

Part 2 Directions: Pretend you want someone to be able to draw the picture you have drawn in Part 1. However, the person drawing the picture cannot see what you have drawn. The person does know shapes (circles, triangles, etc.), so you do not have to explain these. Write directions that describe how to draw the same picture you have drawn.

Directions for drawing my shape picture: _____

_____

_____

_____

Practice
Writing Directions (cont.)

Part 3 Directions: With your teacher's help, find a partner. (If there are an odd number of students, one student may partner with the teacher or with two other students.) Do not let your partner see your geometric picture.

Ask when your partner's birthday is. The person with the earlier birthday in the year gives directions first. Once this is done, it is time for the other person to get ready to draw. The other person draws the picture as the directions are read out loud from the partner's set of directions.

Use the space below to draw the picture. When the directions are finished, compare the picture to the original picture. Then, it is the next person's turn to give directions and the other partner's turn to draw.

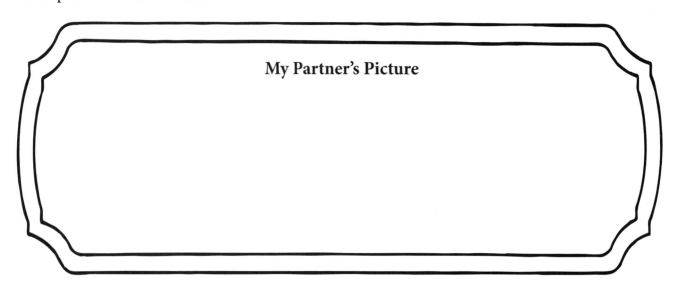

My Partner's Picture

After you have each drawn your partner's picture, answer these questions:

1. How did you do? _____

2. Were the directions well written? _____

3. Did your partner need to do anything to have better written directions? If so, what?

_____

_____

_____

Relay the Directions

Materials Needed: 2 tennis balls, 2 cans or buckets

Directions:

- Divide the class into two equal teams. If there is not an even number of students, ask some students to take turns being the scorekeeper. Be sure to let the students swap out with other students during the different relay races so everyone can participate.

- Students must listen carefully as the teacher gives directions. Remind students that directions will not be repeated.

- Students will stand in straight lines. A bucket or can should be placed at the front of each line.

- The student at the start of each line will be given a tennis ball.

- Students cannot begin until the teacher says "go."

Use the list below to give directions to begin each relay.

Relay List

1. Using only your right hand, pass the tennis ball to the person behind you. When the ball gets to the end of the line, continue passing it back to the front of the line. The last person to touch the ball must put the ball in the bucket or can. The first team to get the ball in the can, while following directions, wins a point.

2. Same directions as #1, but students use only their left hands. The first team to get the ball in the can wins a point.

3. Use both hands and pass the tennis ball over your head to the person behind you. When the ball gets to the end of the line, continue passing it back to the front of the line. The last person to touch the ball must put the ball into the bucket or can. The first team to get the ball in the can wins a point.

4. Use both hands and pass the ball to the next person by bouncing the ball. The person behind you must catch the ball. When the ball gets to the end of the line, pass it back to the front of the line. The last person to touch the ball must put the ball in the bucket or can. The first team to get the ball in the can wins a point.

When Spelling Takes Teamwork

Materials Needed: markers, 3" x 5" index cards (26 per student)

Directions: Divide students into groups of 3 or 4. Give each student a set of 26 index cards. Give students time to write the letters of the alphabet on each set of cards, one letter per card.

The teacher will say a word from the lists below. Students in each group must find the correct letters and hold up the letters in the correct order to spell the word. The letters must be held up so that the final word is where the teacher can see the correct spelling. If a group has spelled a word incorrectly, the teacher will tell the group the word is incorrect, and the group can try again. The first group to show the correct spelling wins a point for their spelling team.

Hint: Add words from a recent spelling list to the lines below.

List 1	List 2	List 3
camera	daffodil	summer
waffle	sandwich	traffic
police	friends	clothes
secrets	adventure	cartoon
vehicle	colony	remote
yellow	tomorrow	robot
pocket	grammar	supper
_____	_____	_____
_____	_____	_____
_____	_____	_____

Answer Key

Page 6 — Follow Directions Effectively

1. A. circle; B. circle with face

2. A. three circles; B. snowman

3. A. sailboat; B. clown face and hat

4. A. house; B. different house

Page 8 — Don't Do This, Don't Do That

At the end of the "do not" directions, everyone will be standing beside his or her desk.

Page 9 — Working with Differences

Answers will vary. Accept appropriate responses.

Page 11 — Taking Artistic Direction

1. *color green*
   color brown
   draw smile
   color yellow
   draw smile

2. *draw tears*
   draw bow in hair
   color hair yellow
   color purple
   color red

3. *color gray*
   color blue
   draw a grin
   draw a moustache
   draw a fishing pole

4. *draw mouths*
   draw hats
   color one hat purple
   color one snowman red
   draw a rabbit

Page 12 — Moving with Symbols

1. Students should be walking.

2. Students should stop.

3. Students should pretend to be walking up stairs.

4. Students should pretend to be swimming.

5. Students should smile.

6. Students should pretend to be fishing.

7. Students should be quiet.

8. Students should pretend to be talking on a phone.

Page 13 — Getting Around the Town

Check student maps for accuracy. Red Xs should be drawn on Maple St. and Cherry Rd.

Directions to the pet store: Take Willow St. to Oak Ave. to Hickory Lane. Turn left on Palm Ave.

Page 14 — Following From "Left" to "Write"

Student directions in parentheses tell where the wad of paper should be placed.

Katie hated eating leftovers (**left hand**) after Thanksgiving, but she knew her family would have leftovers (**on desk**) for several nights whether she wanted them or not. She thought about getting on the computer so she could write (**right hand**) a report for her English class that was due after the holidays. She could write (**on desk**) about why she hated eating leftovers (**left hand**). She could write (**right hand**) about all the clever uses her mother had for the leftovers (**left hand**) of turkey. She could write (**right hand**) about the disgusting leftovers (**left hand**) her mother would serve for breakfast for the next two weeks. Really, she could probably write (**right hand**) and write (**on desk**) and write (**right hand**) for days about eating horrible leftovers (**left hand**). Katie sighed. She did not want to write (**right hand**) about anything. She was so full that she really just wanted to take a nap, but she knew if she took a nap she would wake up hungry. And when she woke up, the only thing her mother would offer for her supper was leftovers (**left hand**)! Katie went ahead and took her nap. As she napped, she dreamed about leftovers (**on desk**) that were chasing her and threatening to eat her! Katie jumped out of bed and went straight to her computer to write (**right hand**). She knew she would have to write (**on desk**) down her dream or she would forget it. She couldn't wait to tell about her dream at supper. She would entertain her family with her crazy dream while they all feasted on leftovers (**left hand**)!

Page 17 — Creating Living Clocks

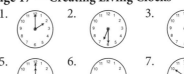

Page 19 — Can You Color the Parts of a Plant?

The flower parts should be colored as follows:

flower — orange   stem — green

leaves — brown   roots — yellow

Page 20 — Listen and Learn About Food Chains

1. Students should take one step forward.

2. Students should not hop.

3. Students should pat their stomachs with one hand.

4. Students should clap three times.

5. Students should take one step back.

6. Students should not sit down.

7. Students should stomp their feet.

8. Students should pat their heads.

9. Students should not wiggle their nose.

10. All students should clap and cheer.

Page 21 — Listen to Directions and Draw

Page 26 — Reading Written Directions

1. Answers will vary.

2. Draw a circle around the answer for number 1.

3. Do not write any answer.

4. Do not draw a picture.

5. Write the date with numbers only.

6. Write the teacher's name on the line; do not write the word "Wednesday."

7. Answers will vary but animals must have four legs.

8. Do not circle an answer.

Answer Key *(cont.)*

Page 27 — Writing Very Urgent Directions!
Accept appropriate responses. The following are possible answers:
1. Go to the office, now!
2. Stop that thief!
3. Stop making so much noise!
4. Clean up this mess.
5. Stop talking in the library.
6. Look out for that slippery spot on the floor!
7. Stop being so mean!
8. Help me!

Page 28 — Following Written Directions for Math
Part 1
Problems 2 (18), 6 (49), 7 (27), 10 (22), and 11 (0) should not be answered.
1. 20   3. 4   4. 16   5. 56   8. 32   9. 48   12. 40

Part 2
Problems 14 (28), 15 (18), 16 (96), 19 (12), 22 (0), and 24 (42) should not be answered.
13. 25   17. 45   18. 20   20. 15   21. 40   23. 55

Page 30 — Paying Attention to What's Written
1. Underline only the lowercase *c*s.
2. Circle the *y*s and *Y*s and trace the word *yak*.
3. Trace the *s*s and *S*s, and the word that is written should start with the letter *s*.
4. Trace the *w*s and *W*s, and the word that is written cannot start with the letter *w*.
5. Trace the *q* and write the letter four more times.
6. Do not do anything.
7. Write the word *grape* three times (before the word *juice* each time).
8. All letters and words should be circled.

Page 31 — Social Studies Information Hunt
With the exception of #4, the questions to the following page should not be answered. The student should write only his or her name in the top right corner of the page and the answer to #4 (*Mayflower*).

1. Jamestown   4. Mayflower   7. Massachusetts
2. Roanoke   6. England   8. Jamestown
3. Virginia

Page 32 — What If It's Different?
Part 1: Students should not do anything.
Part 2:
1. student's first name   3. student's first name
2. student's first name
Part 3:
1. square
2. triangle
3. triangle
4. triangle
5. triangle
6. square
7. triangle
8. square

Page 33 — How Drawing Is Like Writing
Check student drawings for accuracy.

Page 34 — The Earth, the Moon, the Directions
1. B; draw a picture of Earth
2. A; draw four stars to the right of choice "A"
3. B; Mercury, Venus, Earth, Mars
4. A; draw two lines under "its axis"

Page 35 — It's Time to Learn to Follow Directions
All lines should be left blank. The clock at the bottom of the page should be drawn to show the current time.

Page 37 — Coloring the Places of the Past
Color the stable brown.
Color the barKlue.
Color the dry goods store gray.
Color the school house red.
Color the boarding house yellow.

Page 38 — Completing the Pattern
1. 13, 39
2. 11, 55
3. 17, 136
4. 13, 52
5. 12, 24

Page 39 — Herbivores, Carnivores, Omnivores
herbivores: moose, elephant, chicken, giraffe
omnivores: bear, pig
carnivores: lion, shark, alligator

Page 40 — Not What You Want to Do
1. The letter "A" should be written on the line. Each even number should be circled.
2. The name of a month should be written on the line.
3. The number "12" should be written on the line.
4. (See answer for #1.)
5. The word "raccoon" should be written on the line.
6. and 7. Students should stand up and clap three times.
8. The student's first name should be written on the line.
9. (This line will be blank.)
10. A triangle should be drawn in the box.

Page 41 — Following Directions for Measurement
Parts 1 and 2 should not be completed. The words "I read and follow all directions" should be written on the line at the bottom of the page.

Page 42 — Every Word Is a Step on the Stairs
Answers will vary. Accept appropriate responses.